ເລື່ອງຂອງໂຕເລກ

THE NUMBER STORY

SMALL BOOK ONE

ENGLISH - LAO

Numbers Teach Children
Their Number Names

written and illustrated by

MISS ANNA

Early Reader Edition of *The Number Story 1*
Bronze Medal Winner, 2016 Wishing Shelf Book Award

Library of Congress Control Number: 2018902040

Names: Miss Anna, author.
Title: Number story : numbers teach children their number names / Miss Anna.
Description: Portland, OR: Lumpy Publishing, 2018.
Identifiers: ISBN 978-1-945977-69-5| LCCN 2018902040
Summary: The pictures and rhymes present stories which introduce numbers 0-10.
Subjects: LCSH Numeration—English--Lao--Pictorial works--Juvenile literature. | BISAC JUVENILE NONFICTION /
Languages: English--Lao
Classification: LCC QA141.3 .M57 2018 | DDC 513—dc23

Publisher: Lumpy Publishing
Website: www.missannabooks.com
Email: missanna@missannabooks.com
Facebook: Miss Anna Lumpy

Paperback: ISBN 978-1-945977-69-5
Printed in the U.S.A.   1 3 5 7 9 10 8 6 4 2

Want to learn our
number names?

It is very easy and a lot of fun!

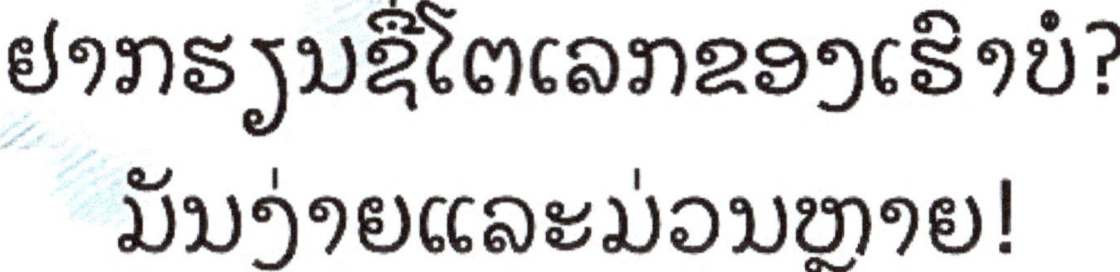

ຢາກຮຽນຊື່ໂຕເລກຂອງເຮົາບໍ?
ມັນງ່າຍແລະມ່ວນຫຼາຍ!

Say-along our little jingle

ເວົ້າຕາມພວກເຮົາ!

starting from Number One!

ມາເລີ່ມຈາກເລກໜຶ່ງ!

1

ONE looks like my one finger.

໑ ✩ ໜຶ່ງ

ມັນຕັ້ງກ້ວຄືນິ້ວມືຂອງຂ້ອຍ

ONE!
ໜຶ່ງ

2
TWO   trails a tail.
໒ ສອງ
ມັນມີຫາງ

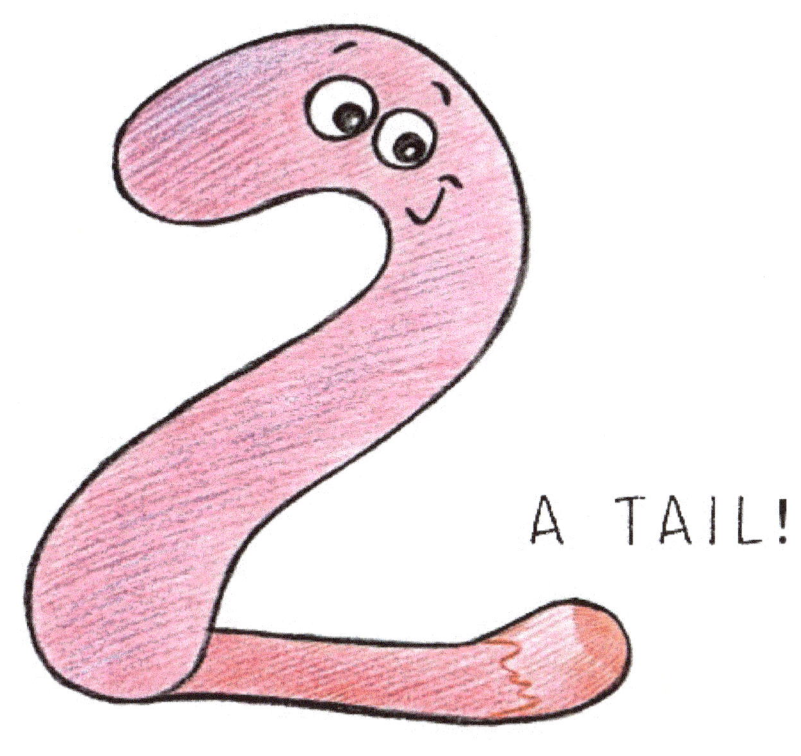
A TAIL!
ຫາງງ!

3

THREE   has bumps.

໓ ✶ ສາມ

ມັນແມ່ນພູເຂົາໂຄ້ງ

ແມມເບິ່ງພູເຂົາຂາວ!

4

FOUR   carries a sail.

໔ ★ ສີ່

ມັນແມ່ນເຮືອໃບ

A SAIL!
เรือใบ!

5

FIVE   is a racing track.

໕ ⋆ ຫ້າ

ມັນແມ່ນຫຼະຫນົນສໍາລັບແຂ່ງລົດ

VROOM!

6

SIX   curves like a snail.

໖ ⋆ ຫົກ

ມັນແມ່ນຫອຍທາກ

A SNAIL!

7

SEVEN has a sharp angle.

ກ ເຈັດ

ມັນມີມຸມແຫຼມຄືກັນມຸມໜຶ່ງ

OUCH!
ອຶ້ຍ!

8
EIGHT   is rollercoaster rails.
໘ ⋆ ແປດ
ມັນແມ່ນລິດໄຟເຫາະຕີລັງກາ

ยิปปี้!
YIPPEE!

9

ລ ☆ ເກົ້າ

ມັນແມ່ນພ່ອງອາກາດອັນໜຶ່ງ
ຢູ່ເທິງແທ່ງໄມ້

A BUBBLE!

ຟອງອາກາດ!

10

TEN is an eye of a whale.

໑໐ ສິບ

ມັນແມ່ນໜ່ວຍຕາດຽວຂອງປາວານ

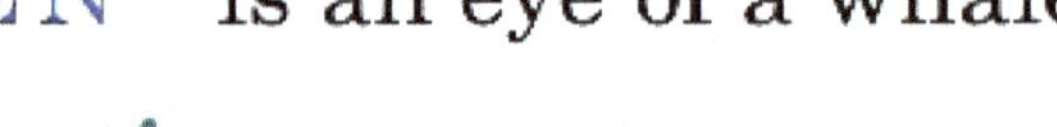

วິ້ງ!
WINK!
HELLO! ສະບາຍດີ!

And
ແລະ

0

ZERO   is an empty pail.

0 ✦ ສູນ
ມັນແມ່ນຖັງເປົ່າ

IT'S
EMPTY!
ມັນວ່າງເປົ່າ!

Thank you for playing with us today.

We had a lot of fun too!

ຂອບໃຈທີ່ຫຼິ້ນກັບເຮົາໃນມື້ນີ້

ພວກເຮົາມ່ວນຫຼາຍ!

We are your Number friends,
Zero to Ten,
Who will be here for you~

ພວກເຮົາແມ່ນໝູ່ຂອງເຈົ້າ
ສູນຮອດສິບ
ພວກເຮົາຈະຢູ່ກັບນ໌ລວຂ້າງເຈົ້າ!

Bye-bye now!
See you again soon!

ລາກ່ອນ!
ແລ້ວພົບກັນໃໝ່!

The Numbers are *SINGING* too!

To sing-a-long, look for Miss Anna Number Story
at your favorite music store like iTUNES.

MP3

Numbers 0-10
IDENTIFYING
& COUNTING

Numbers 11-20
& Ordinals
first, second, third...

Numbers 0-100
& Place Values
ones, tens, hundreds...

About Clocks
& Telling Time
hours, minutes, seconds

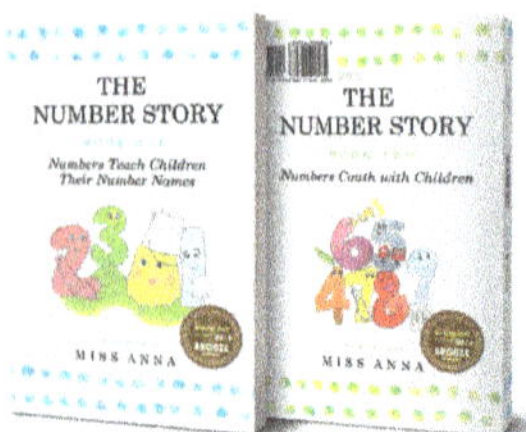

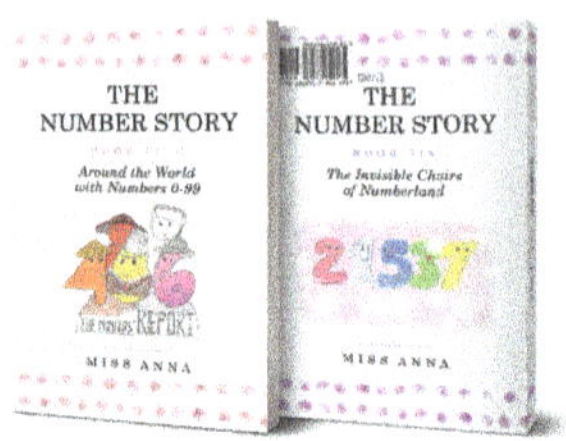

Number Story 1 & 2
isbn: 978-0-996216-48-7

Number Story 3 & 4
isbn: 978-1-945977-01-5

Number Story 5 & 6
isbn: 978-1-945977-06-0

Number Story 7 & 8
isbn: 978-1-949320-40-4

For more Miss Anna books to love,
visit us at

www.missannabooks.com

Numbers are working hard all over the world!
Come Travel the World with Us!